AF478859

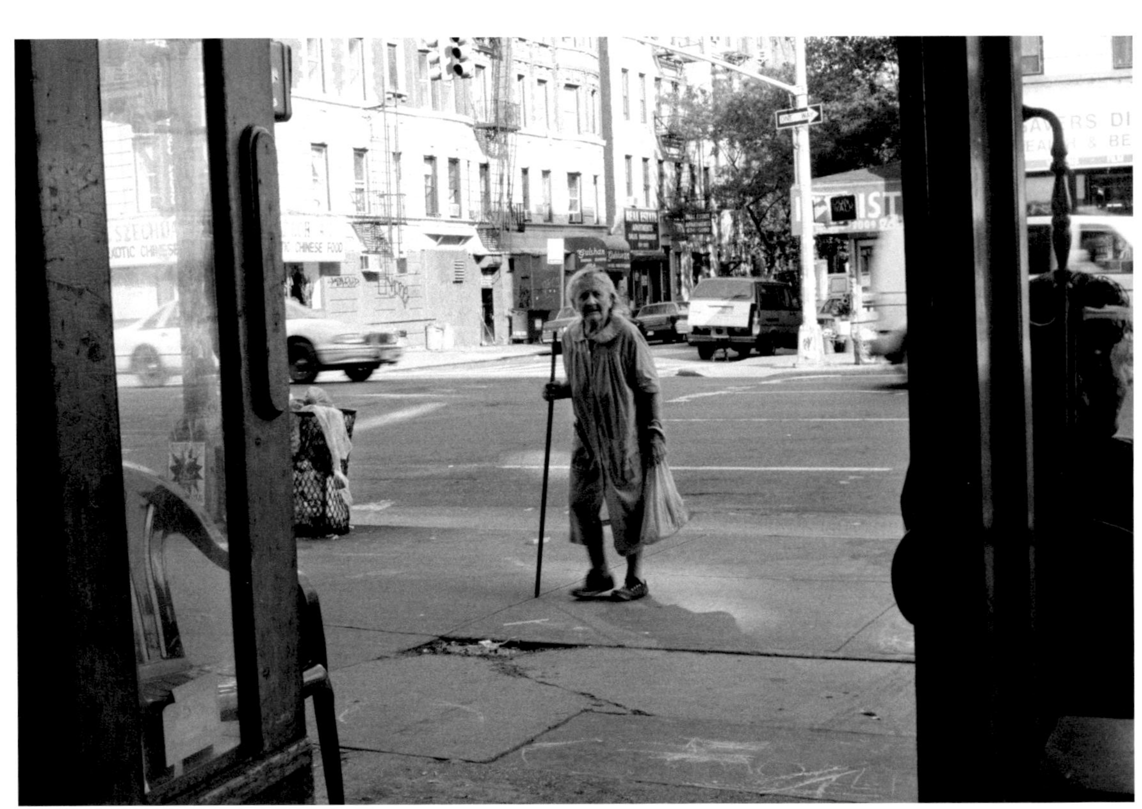

WHERE THE DAY TAKES YOU

By Chrissy Piper

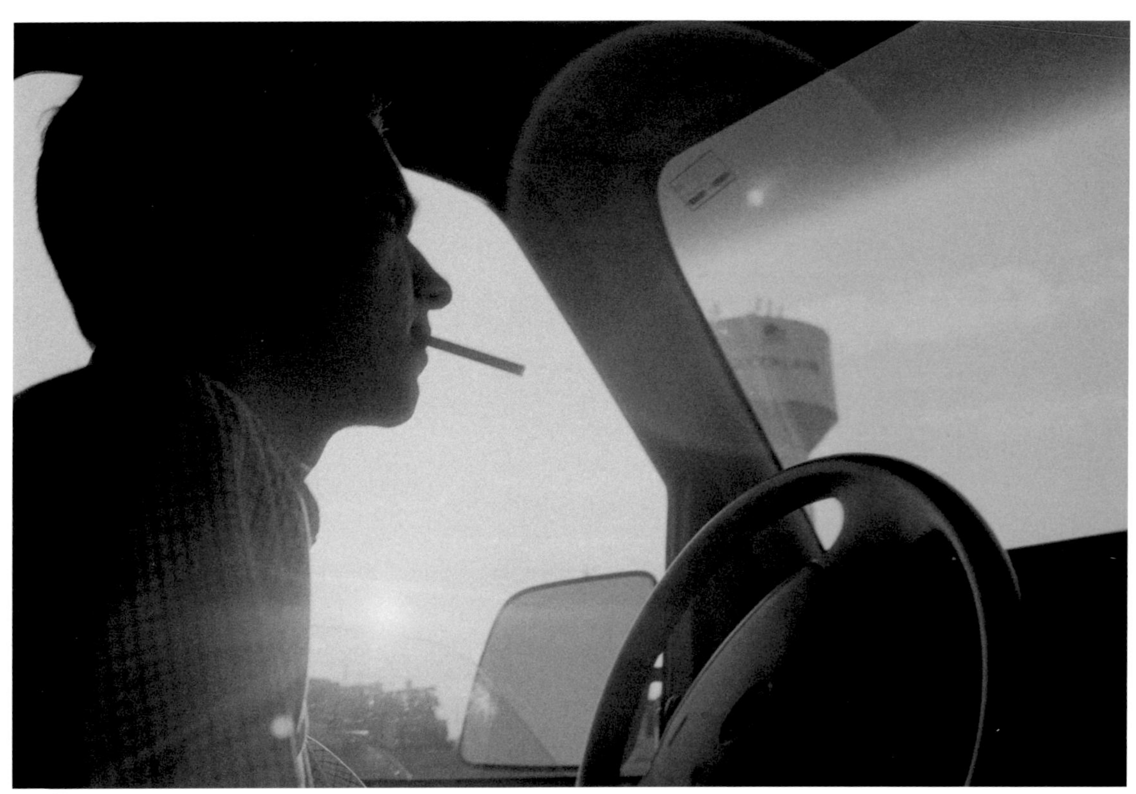

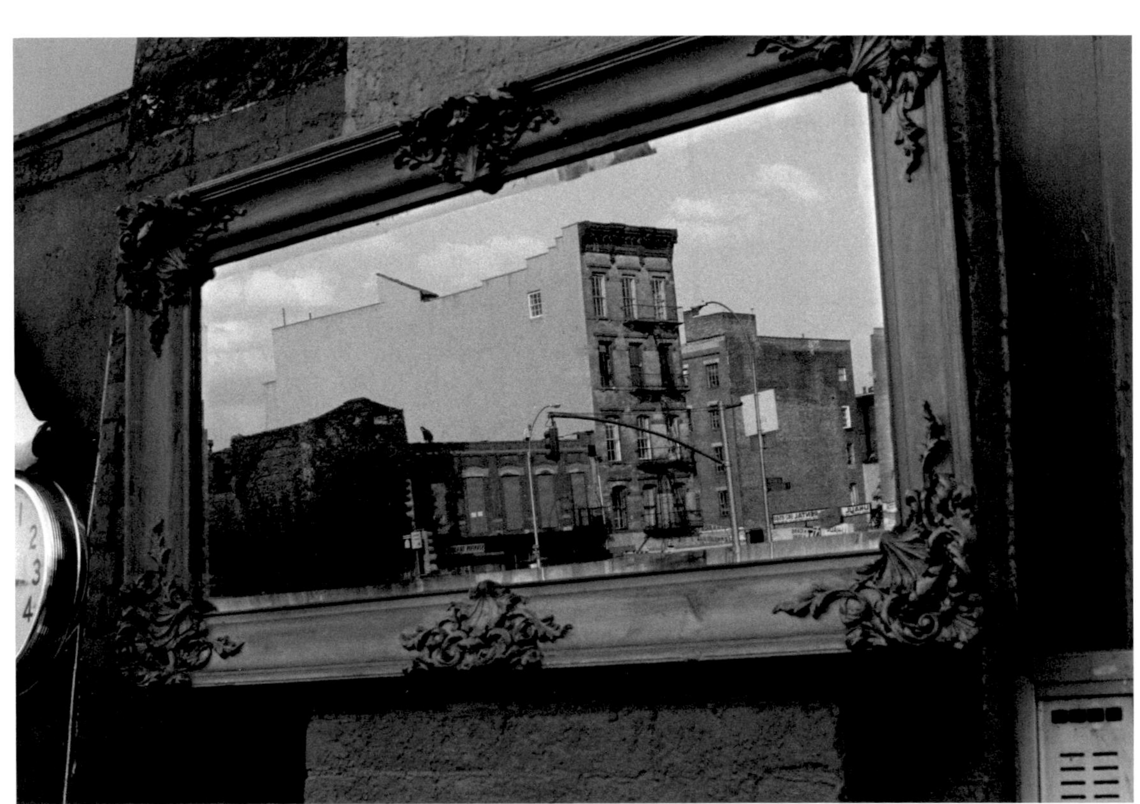

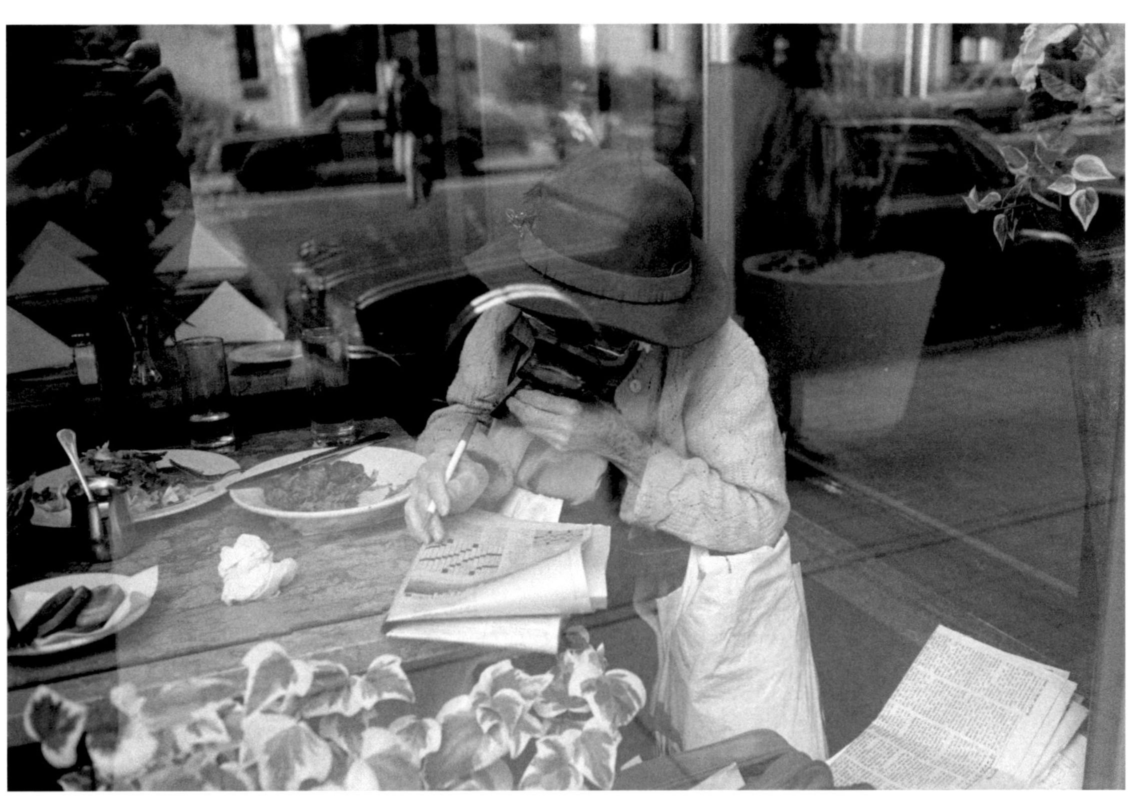

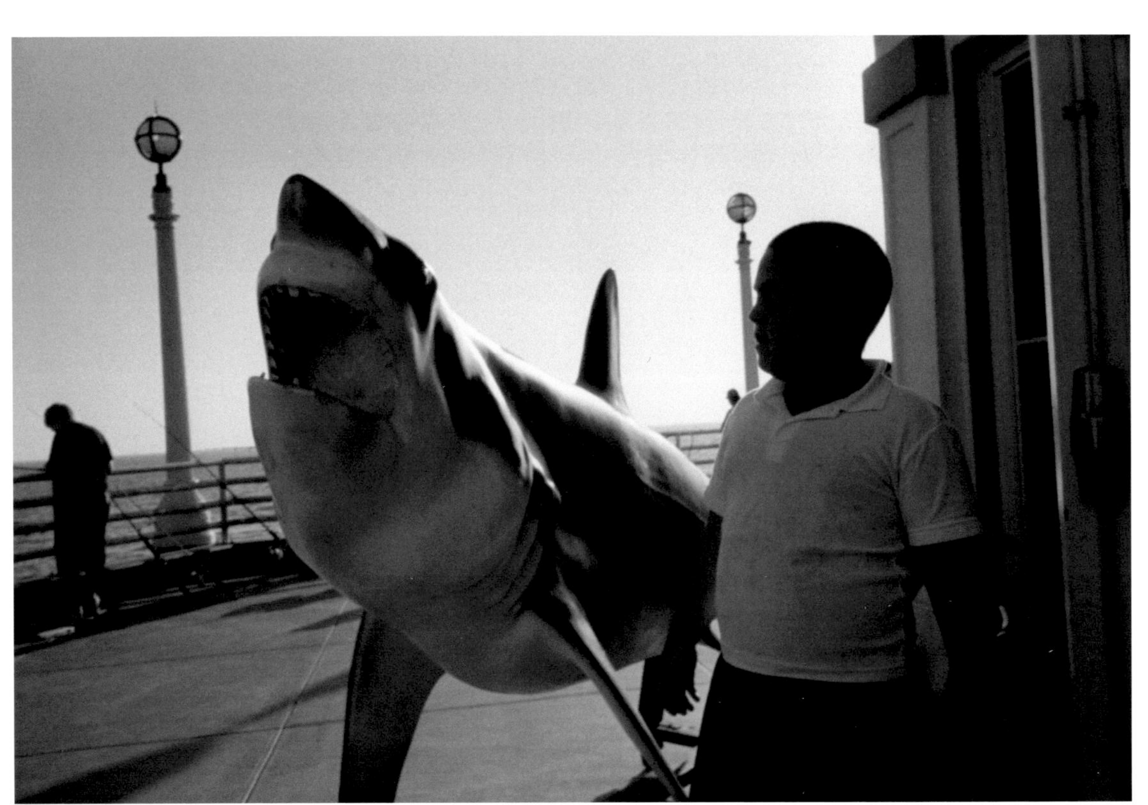

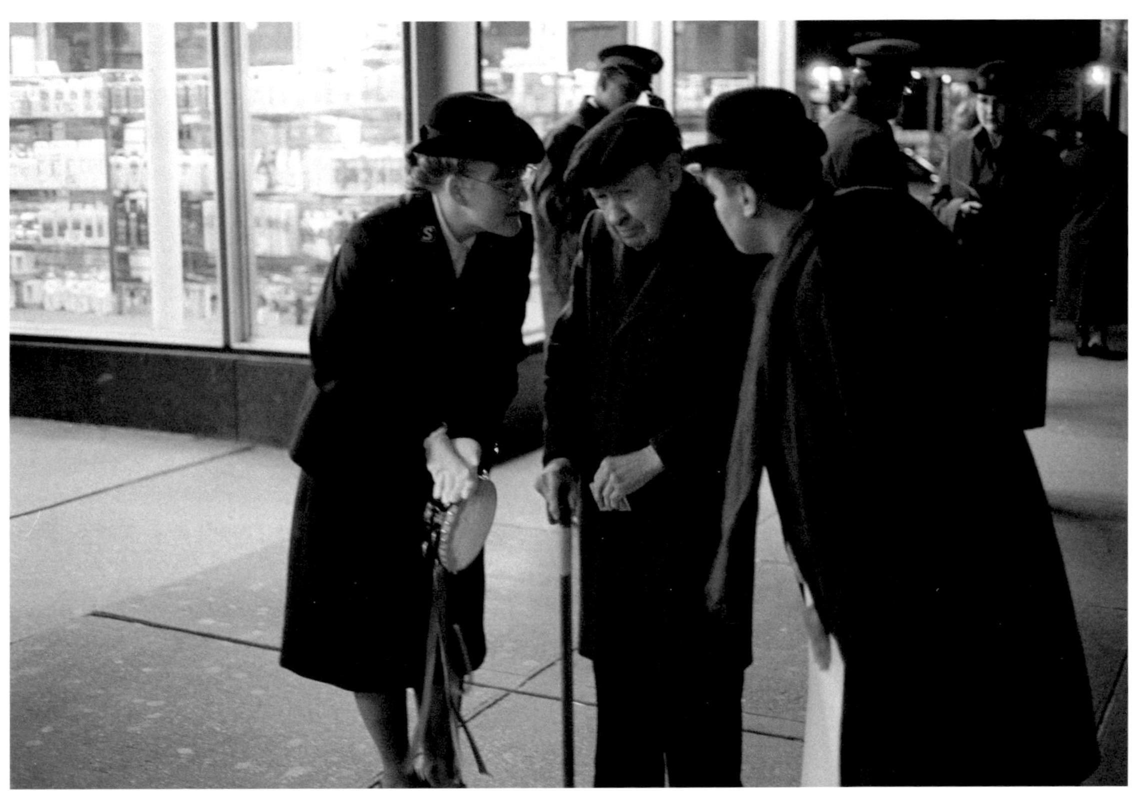

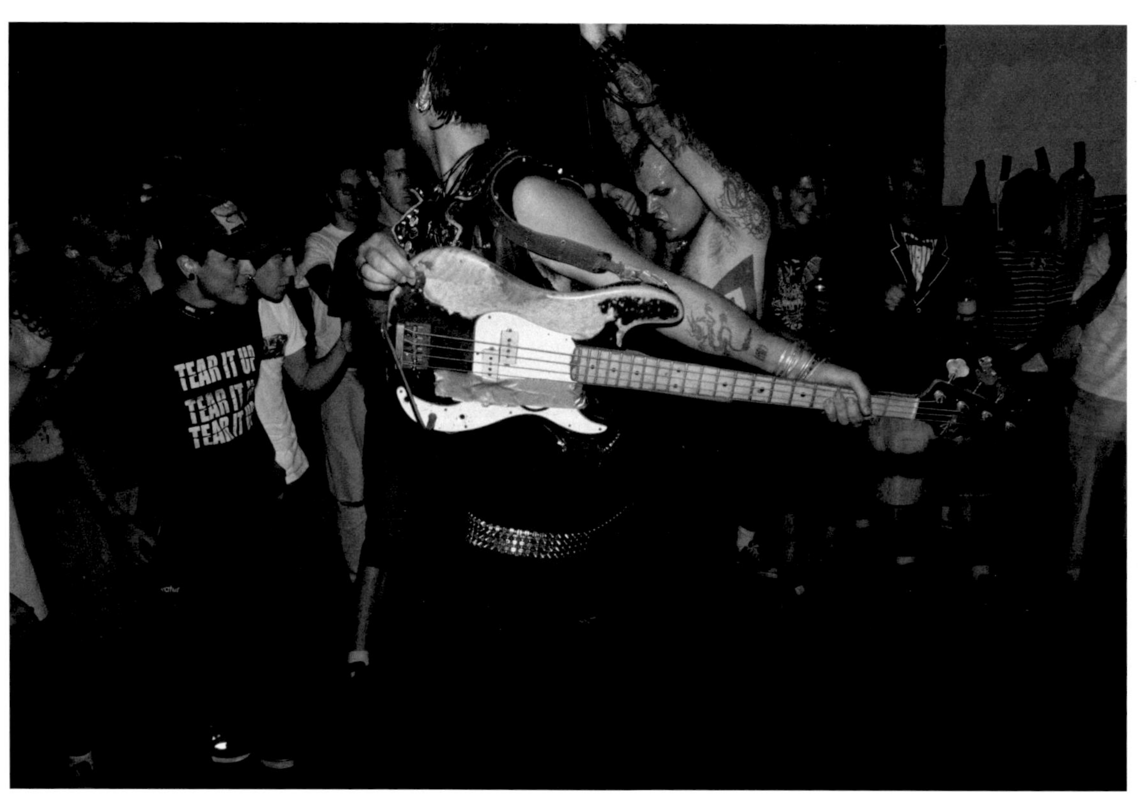

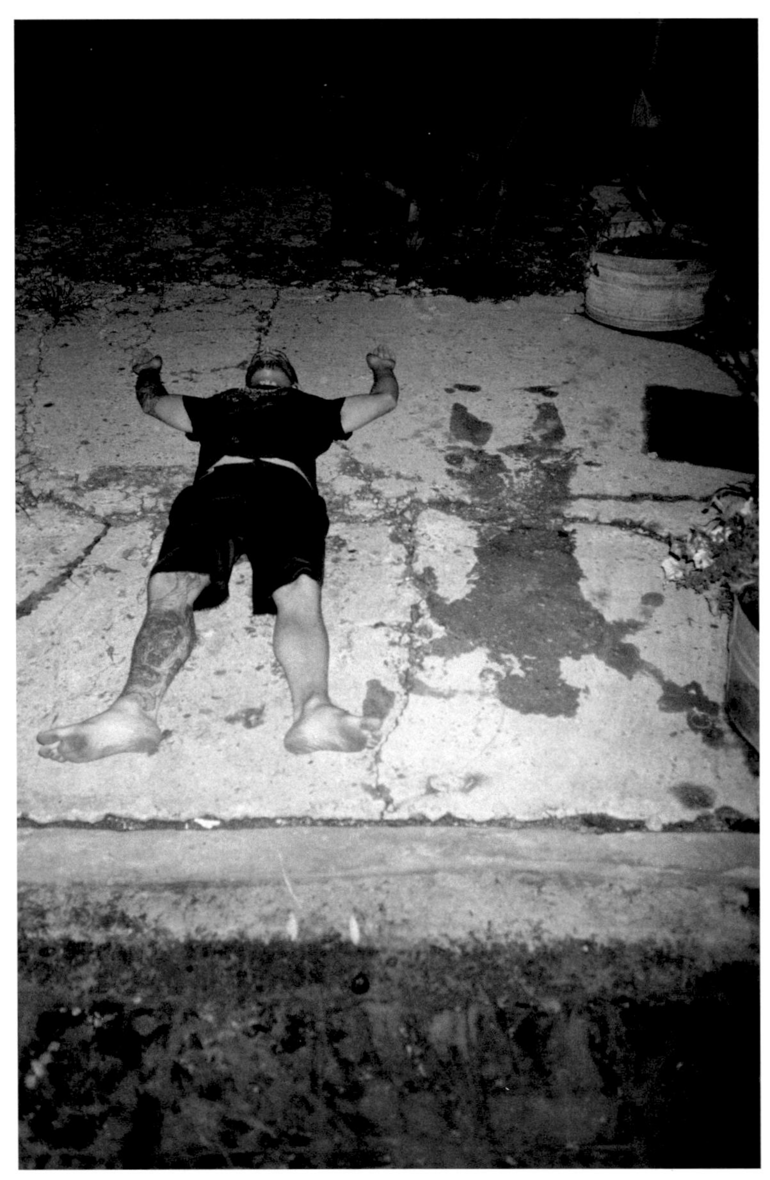

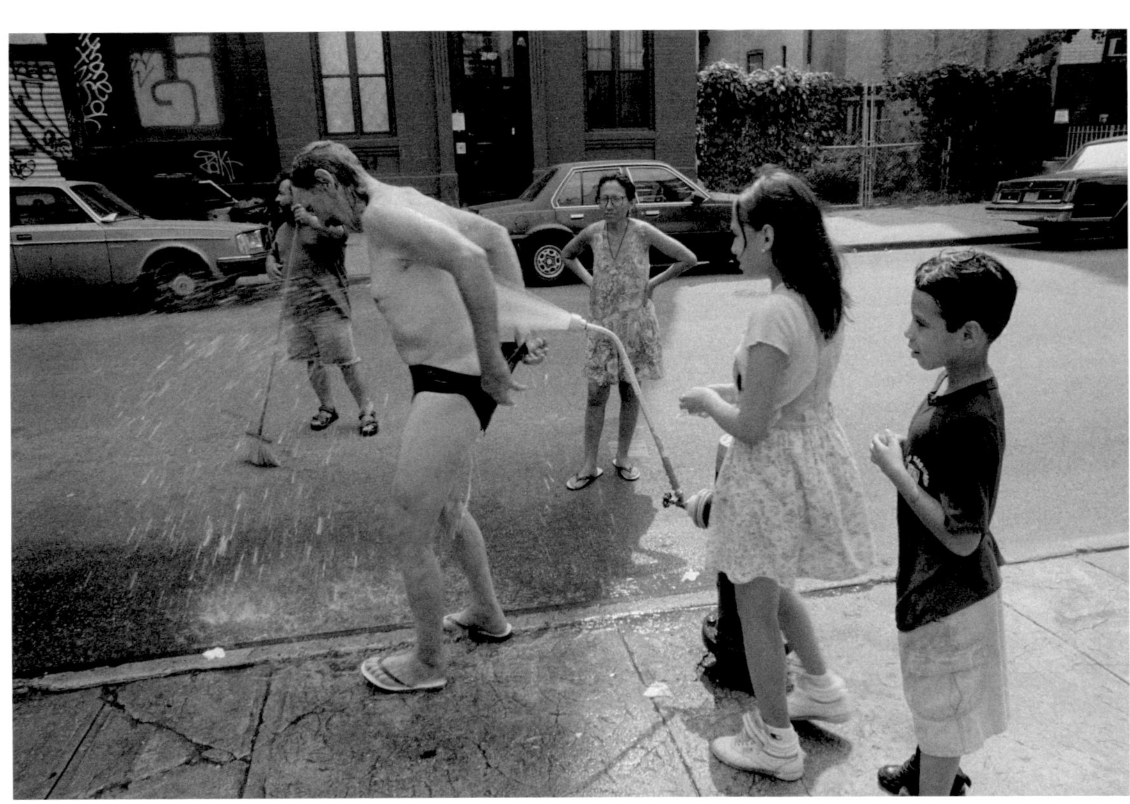

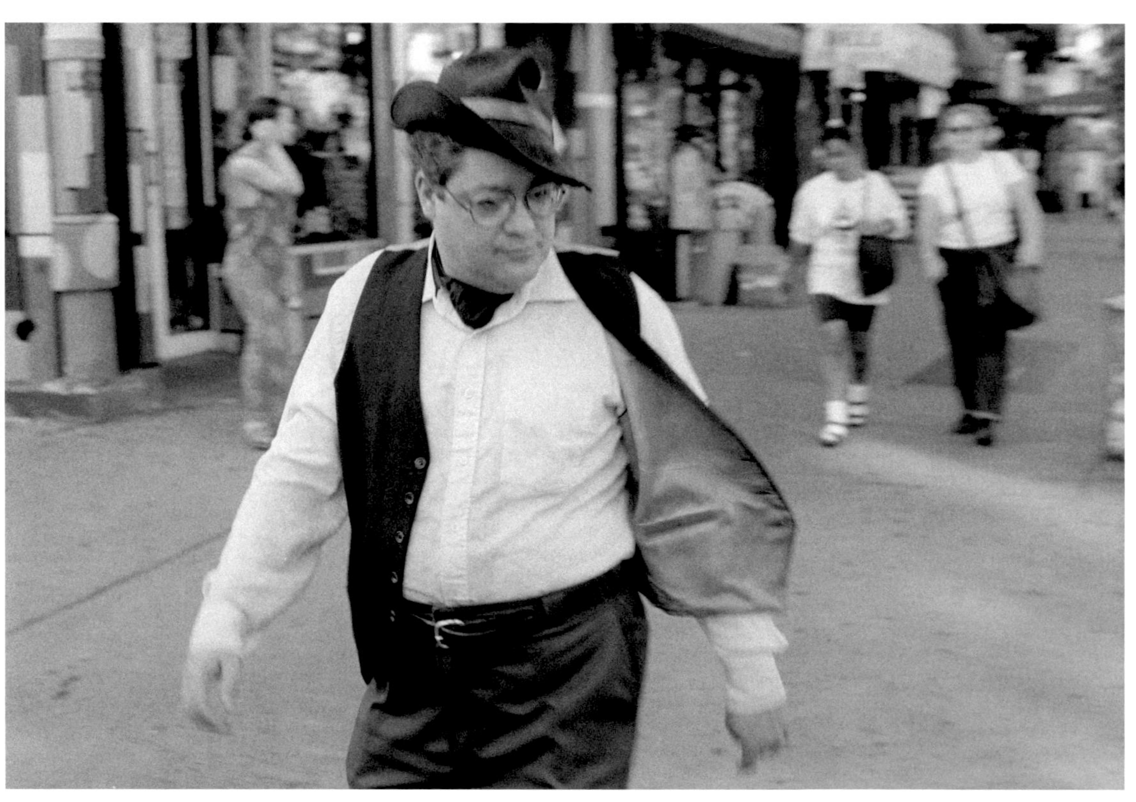

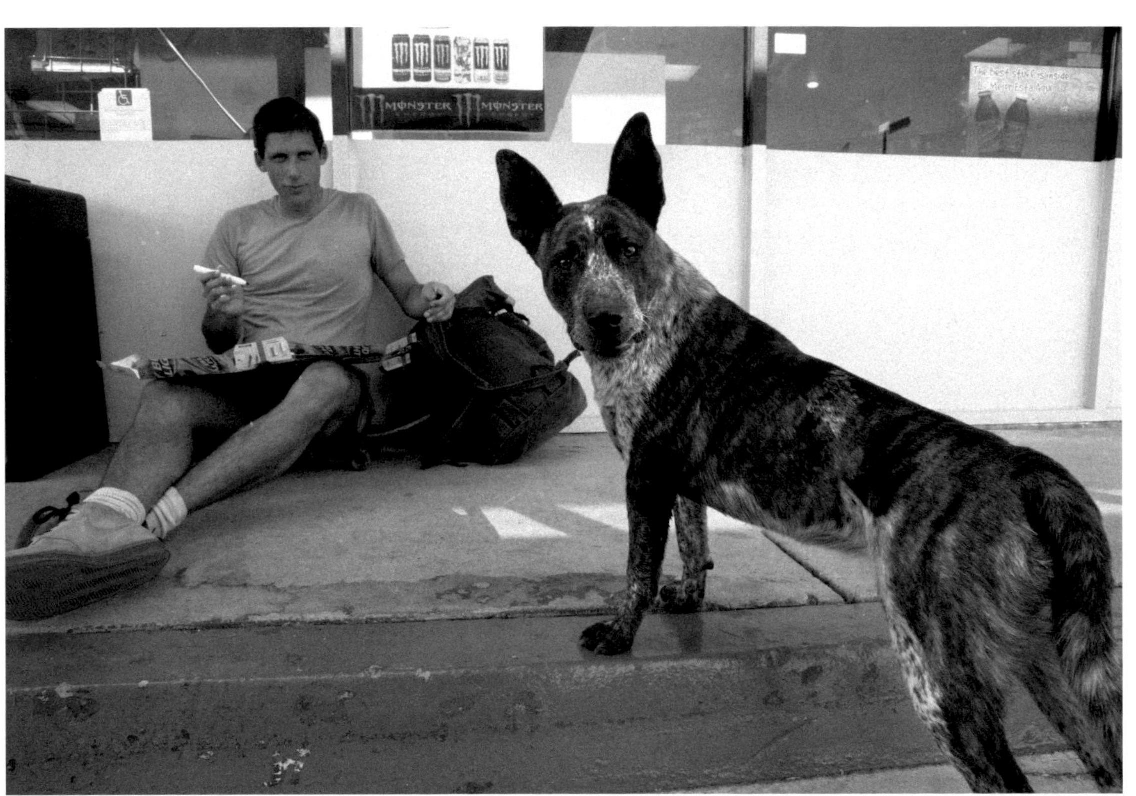

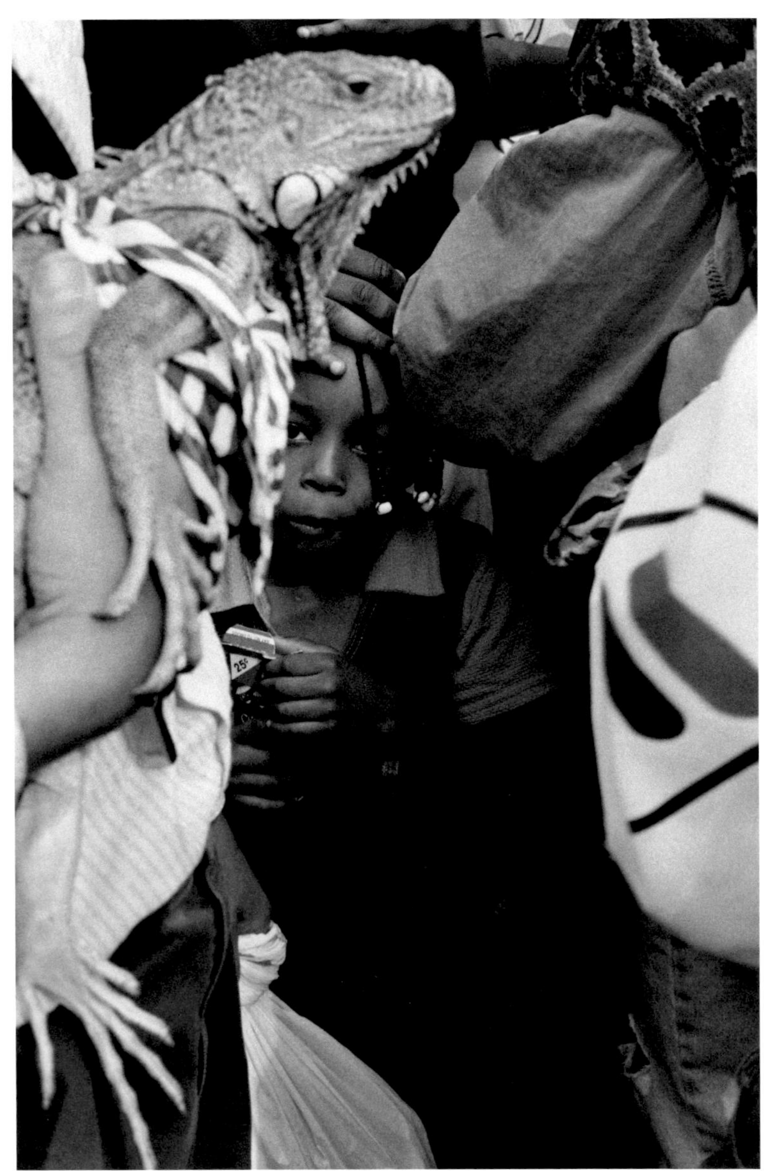

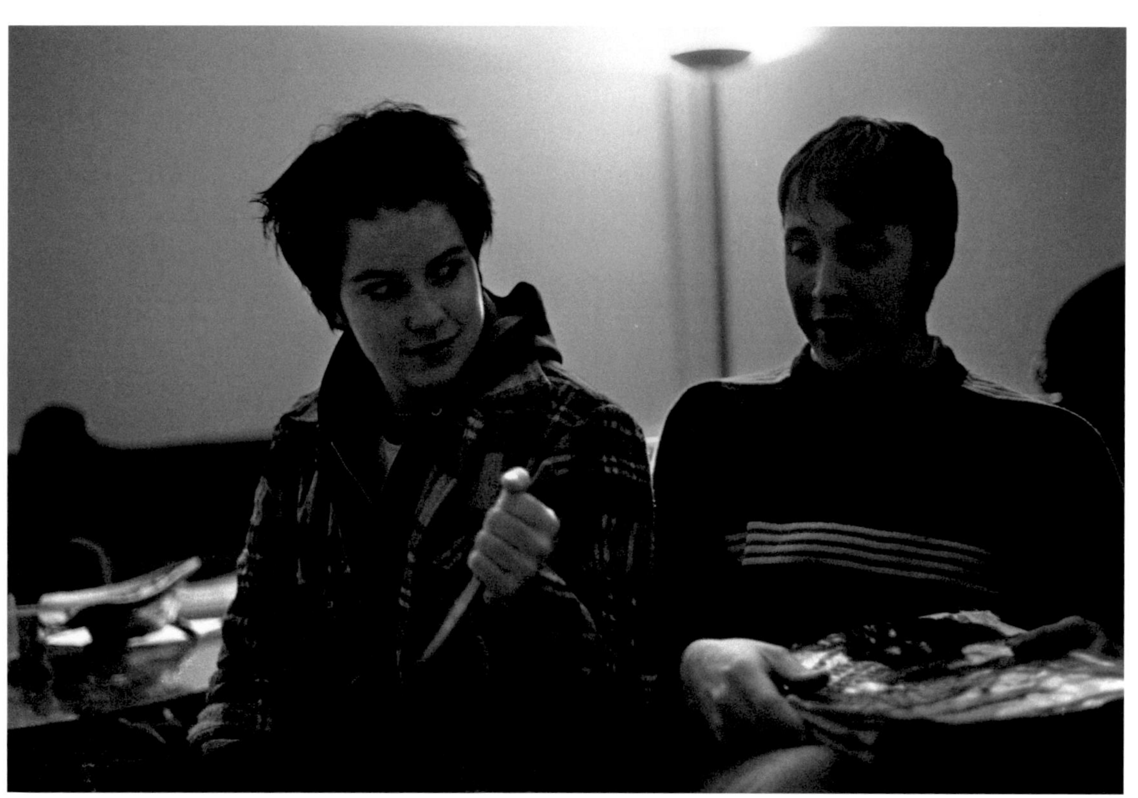

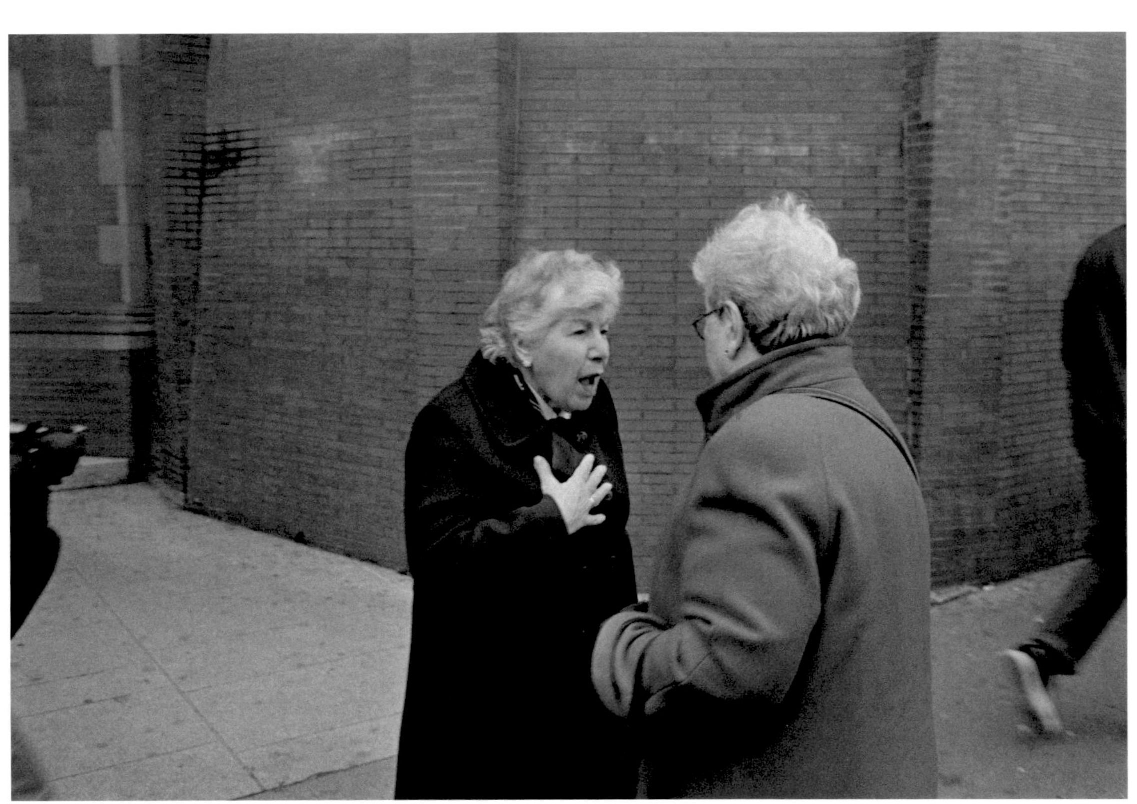

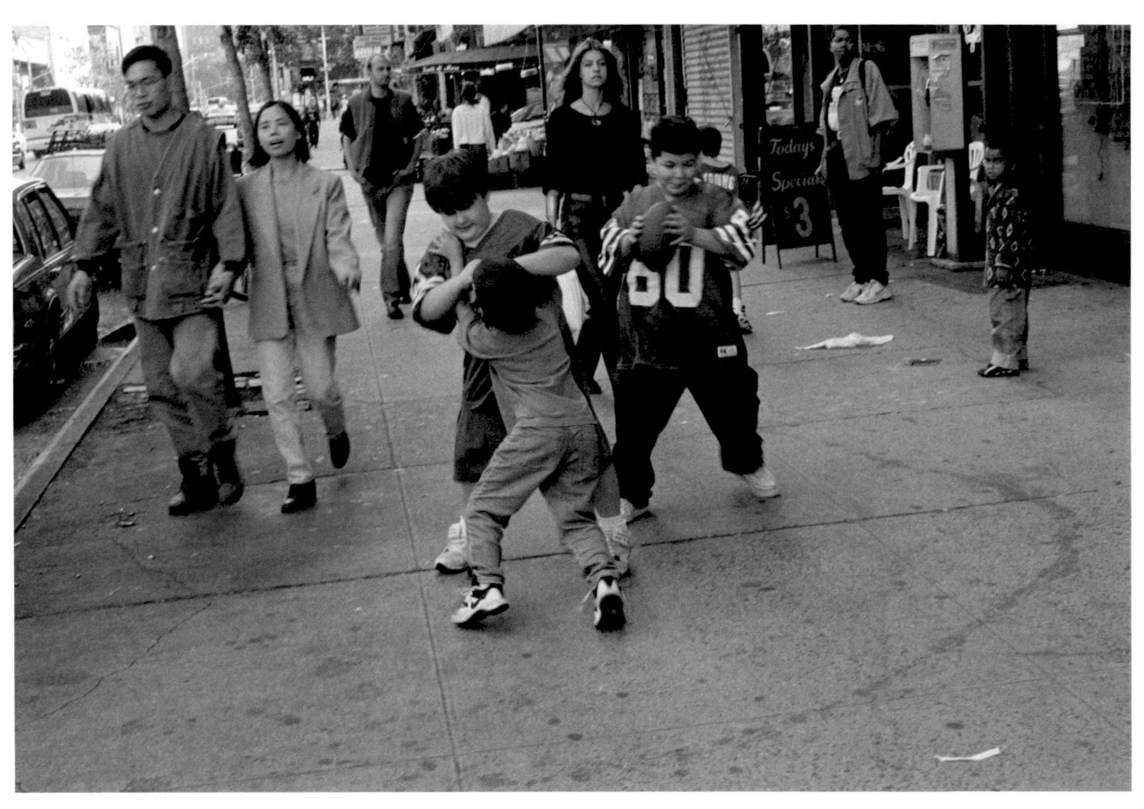

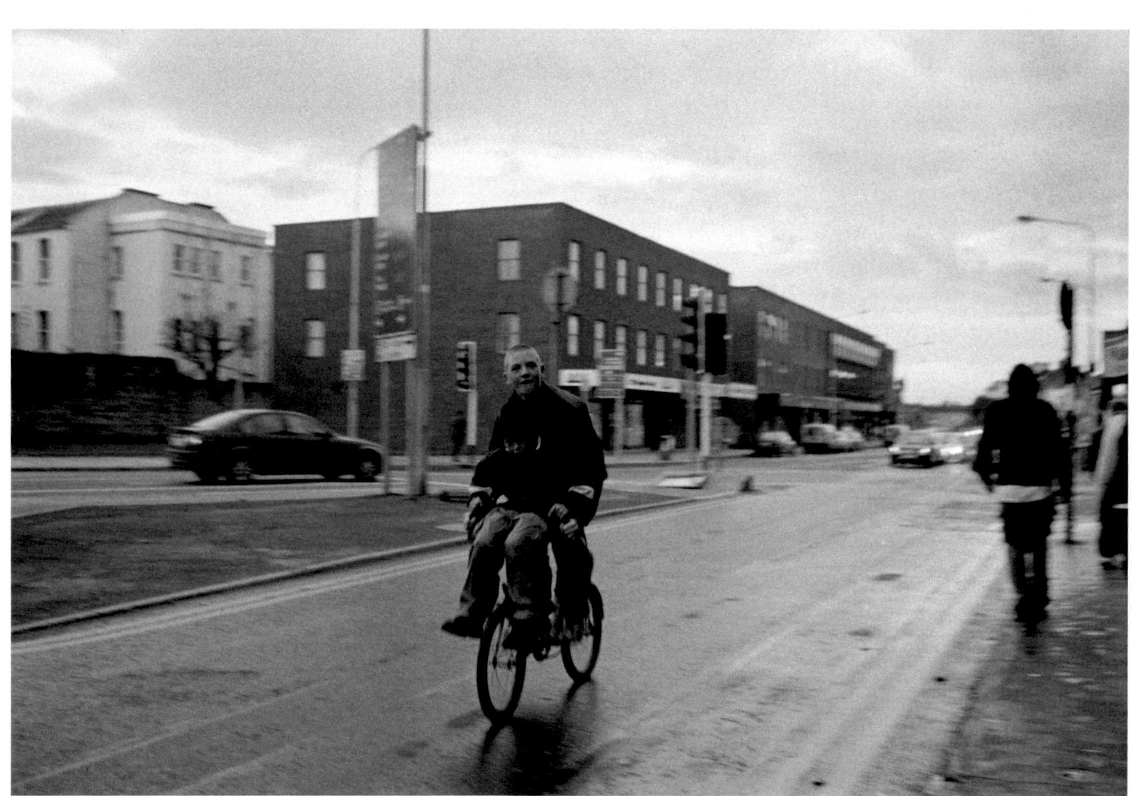

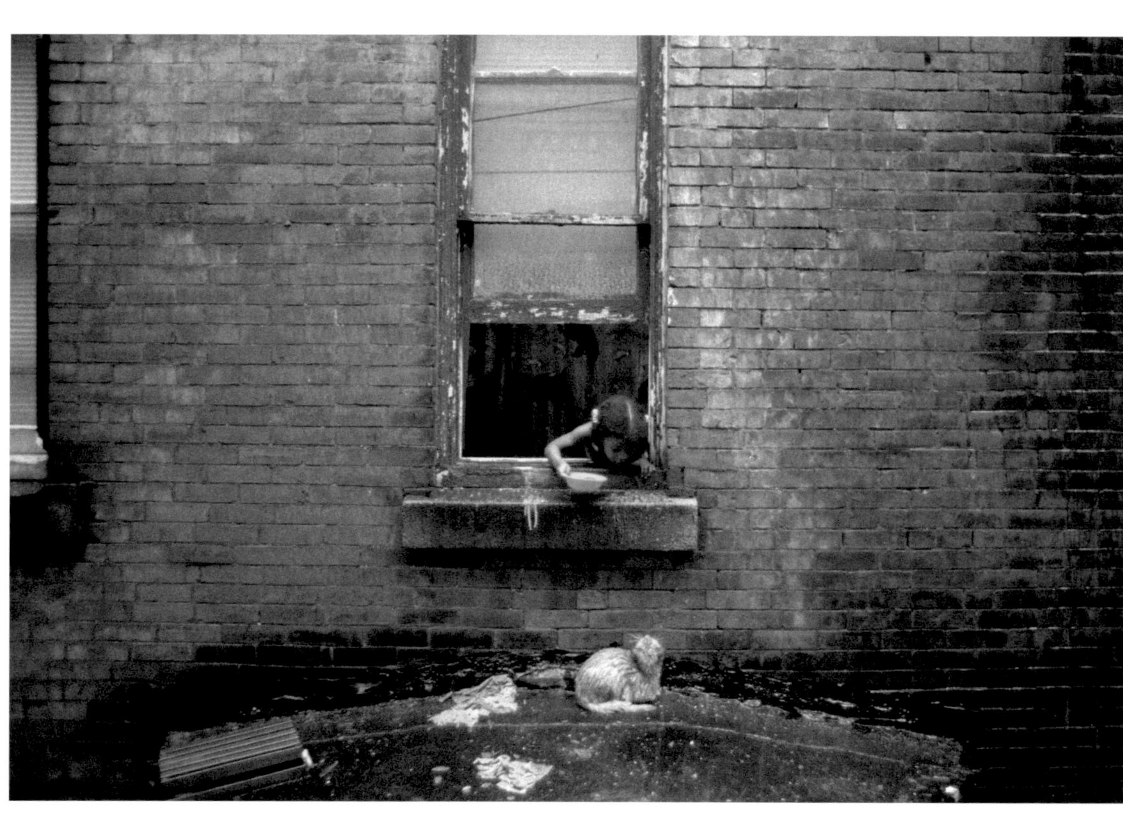

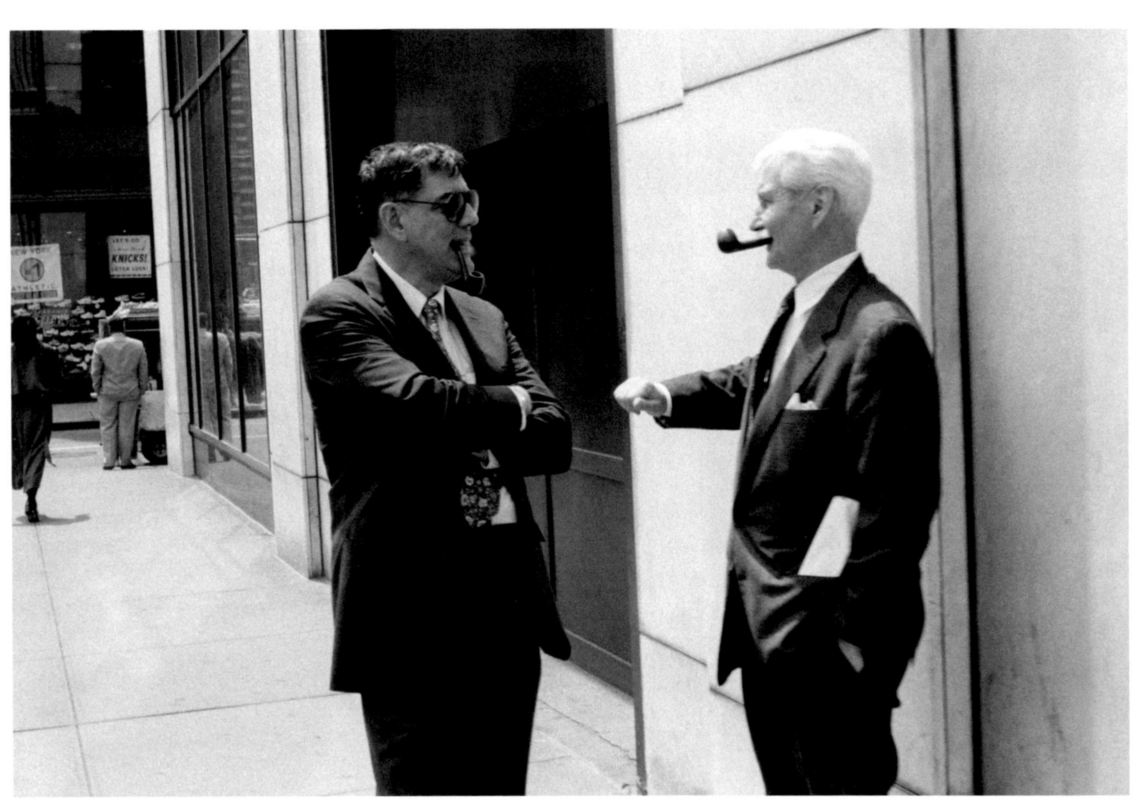
LET'S GO
KNICKS!
LET'S GO
NEW YORK
ATHLETIC

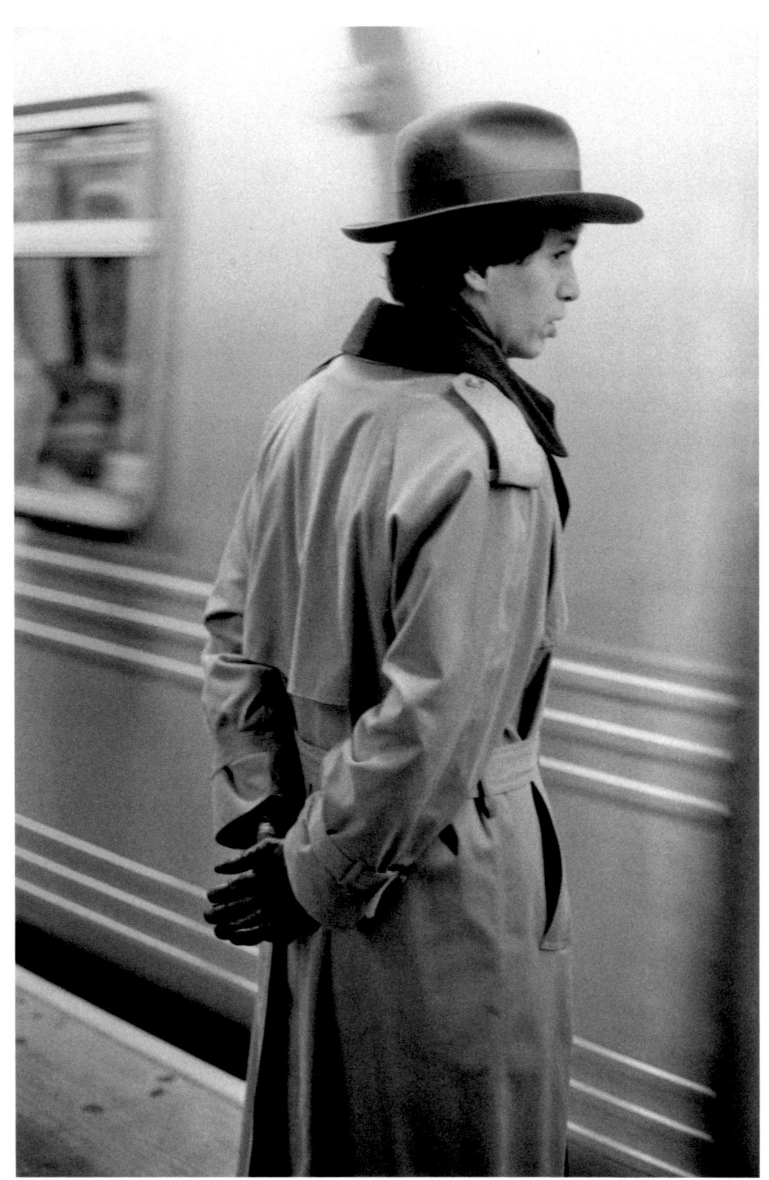

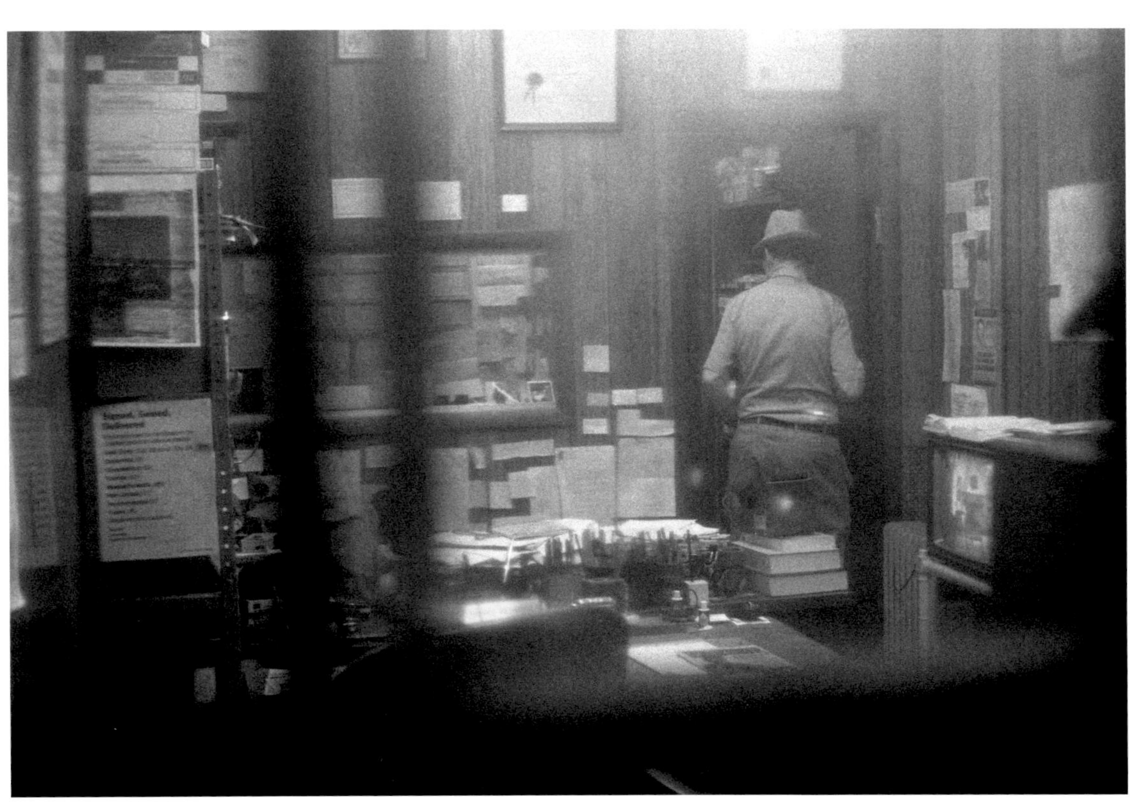

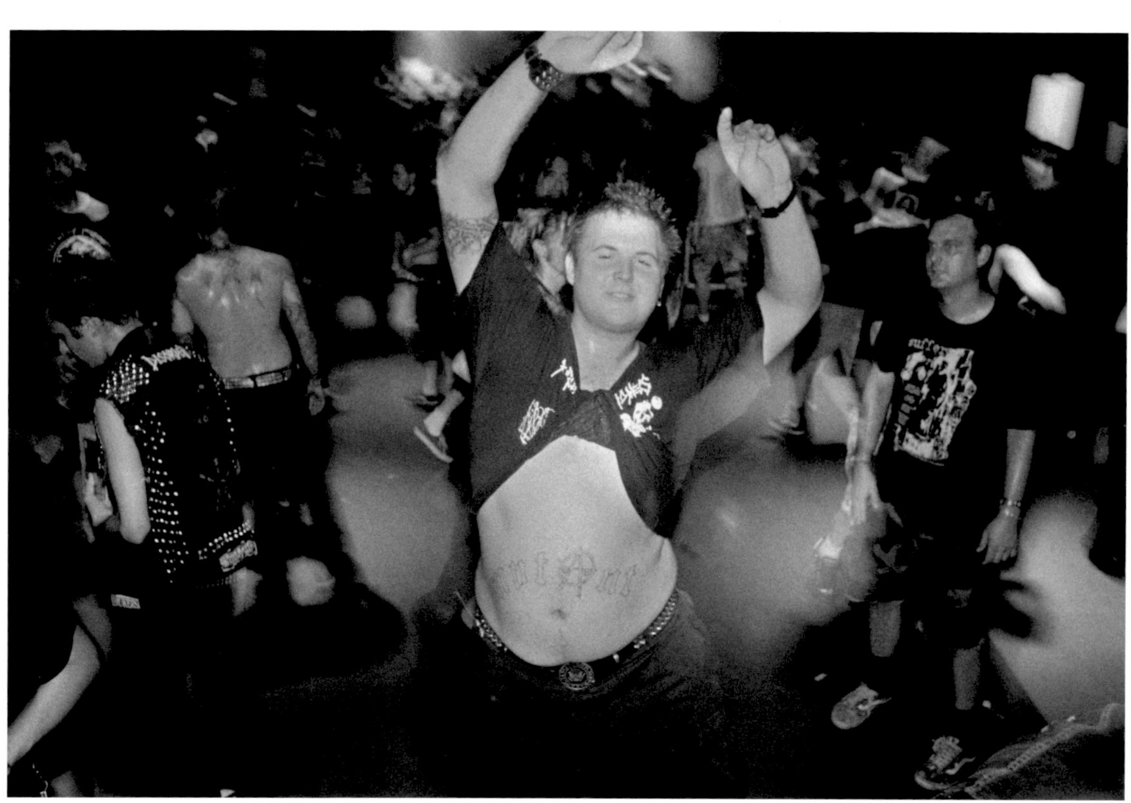

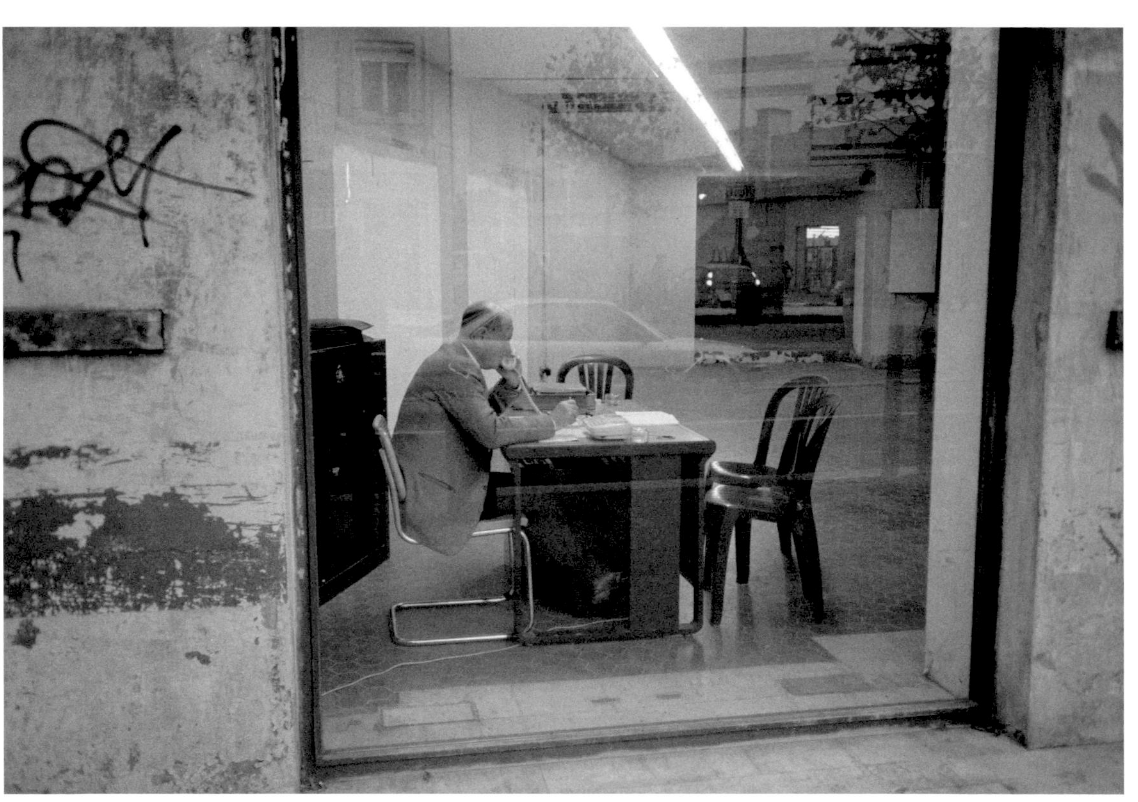

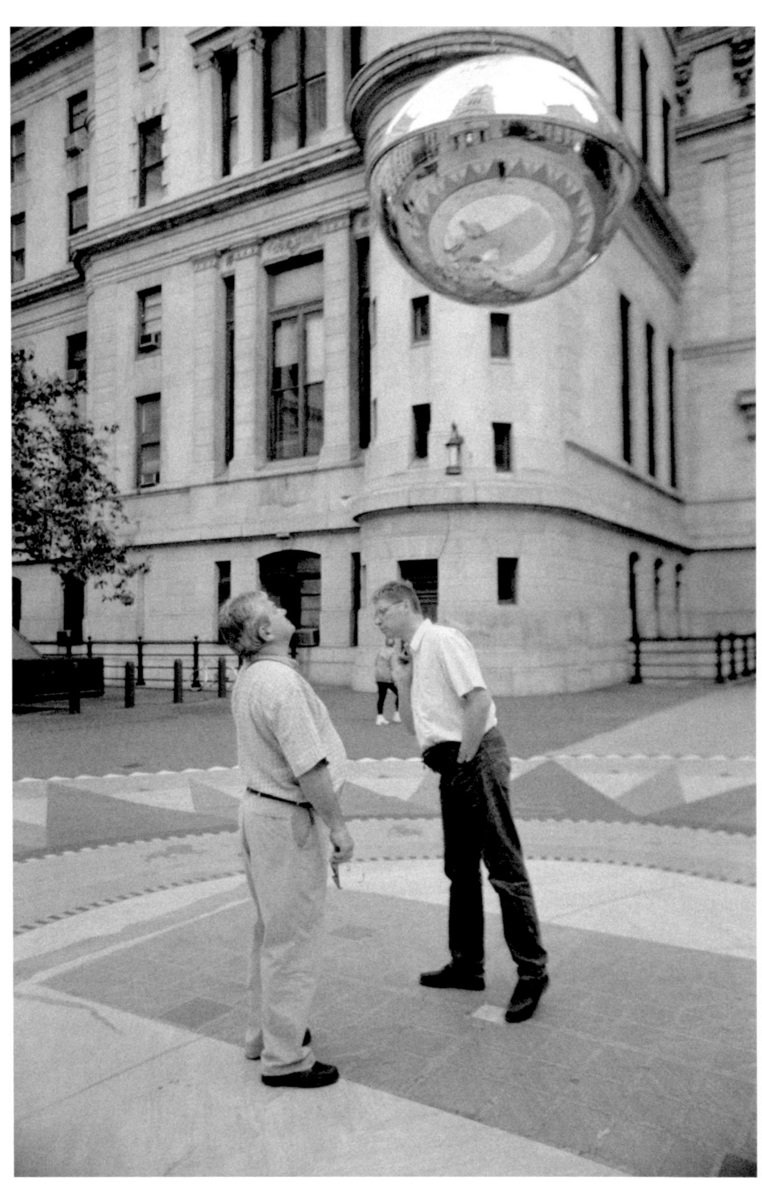

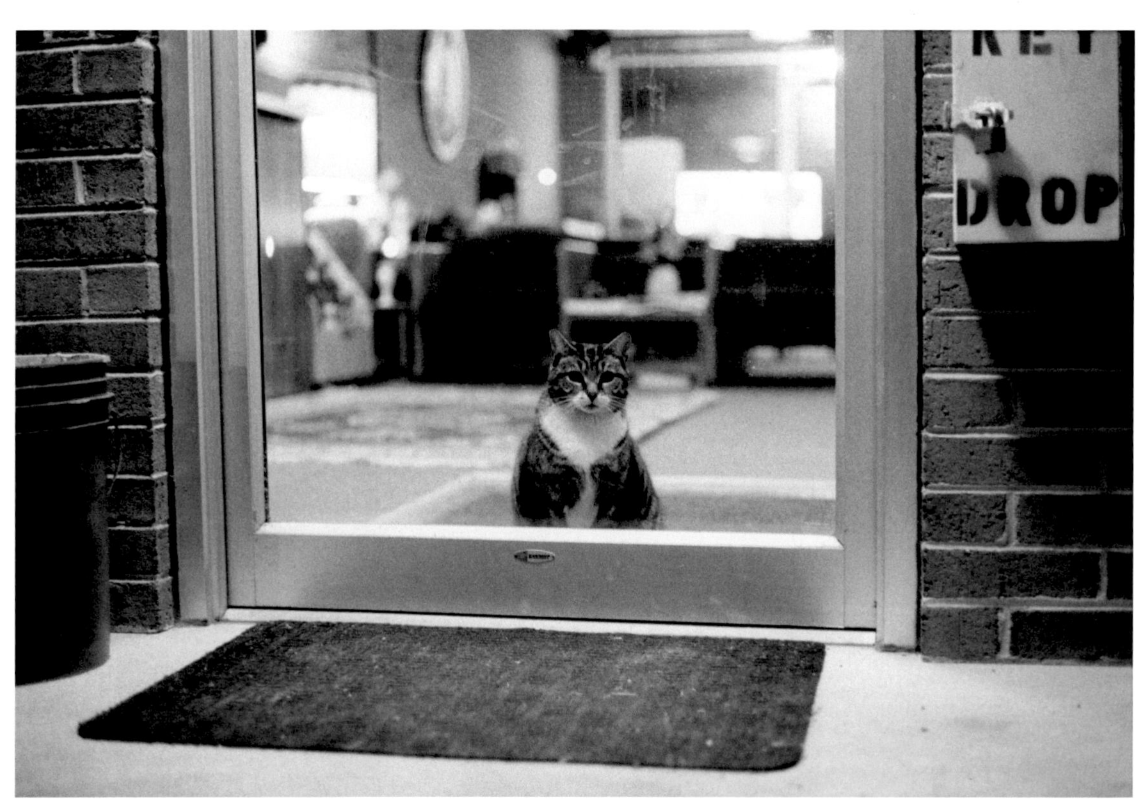
KEY
DROP

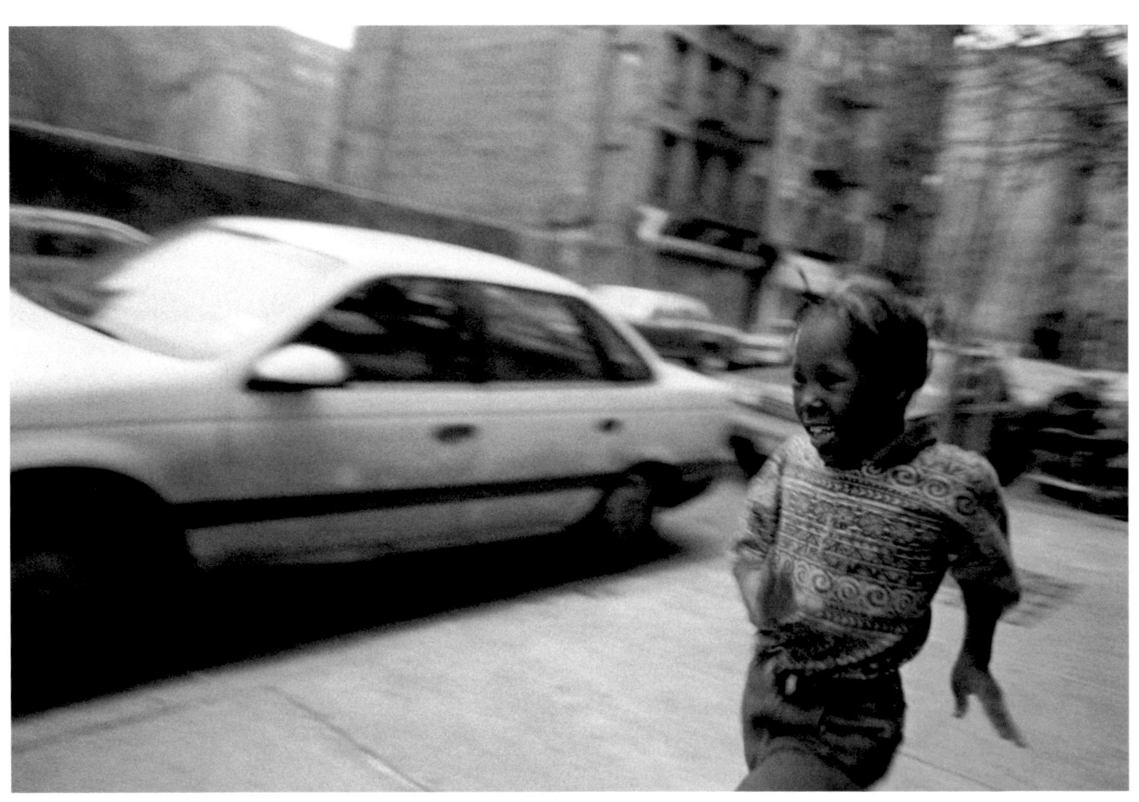

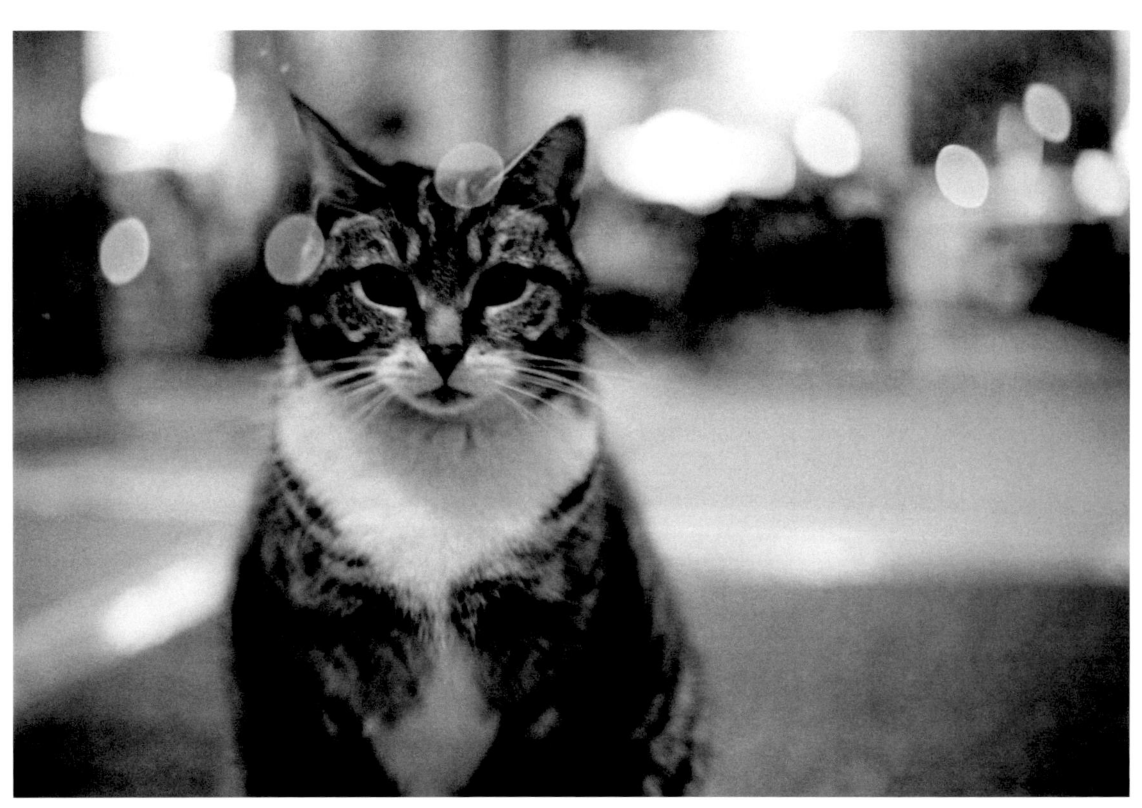

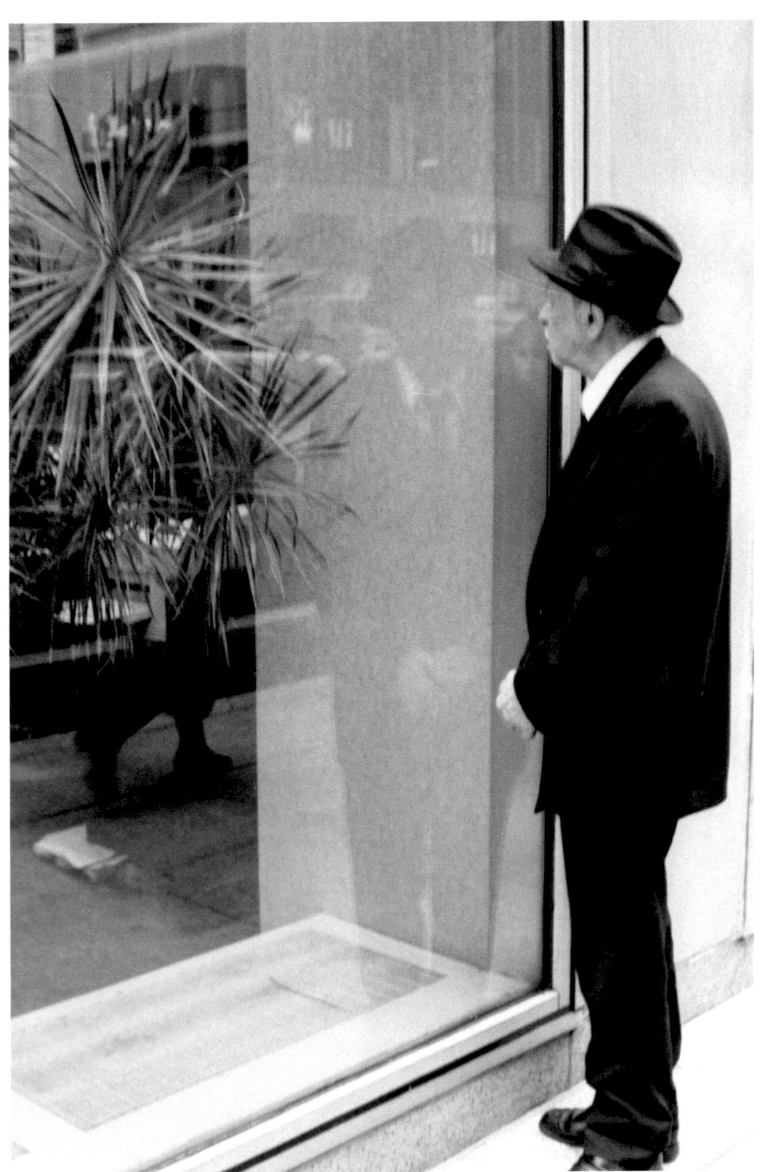

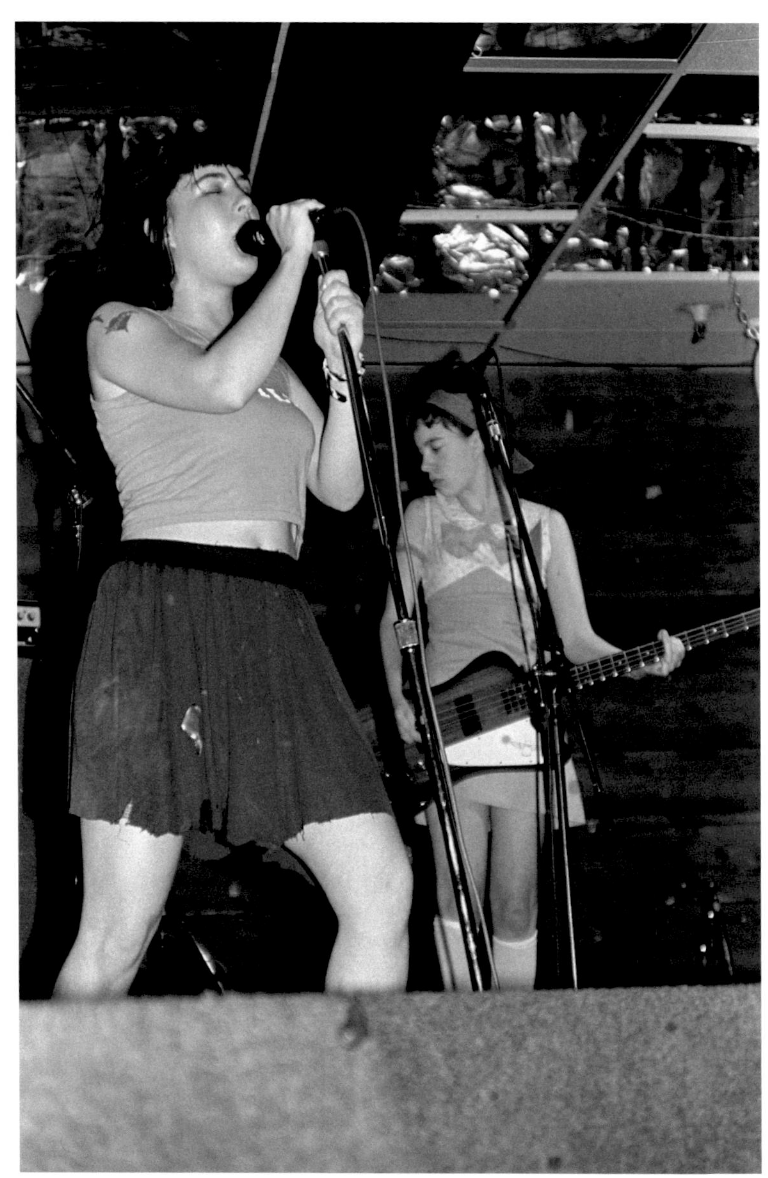

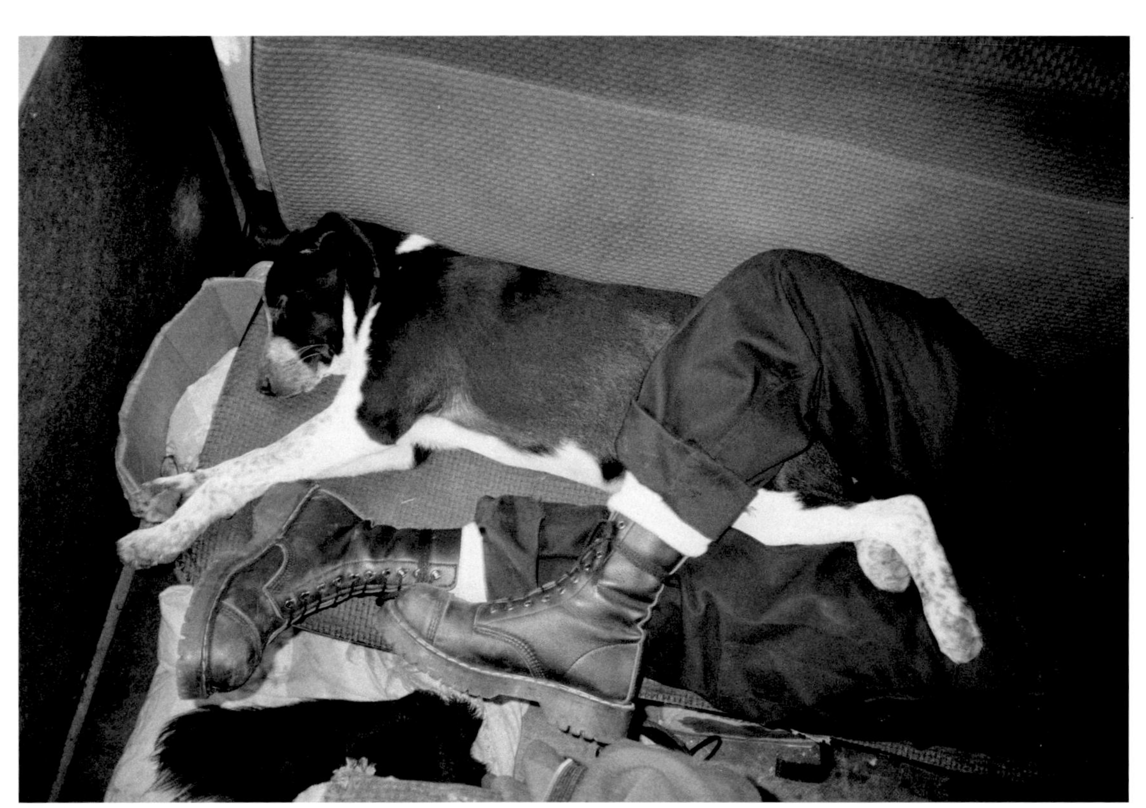

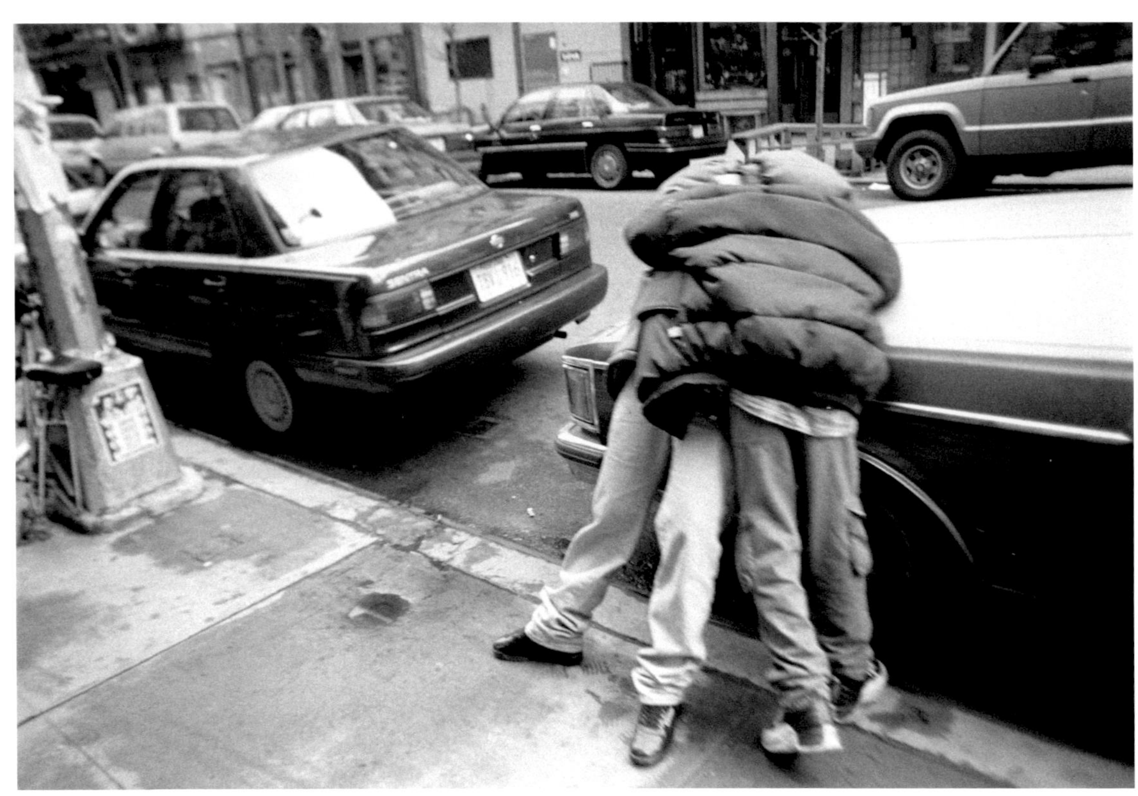

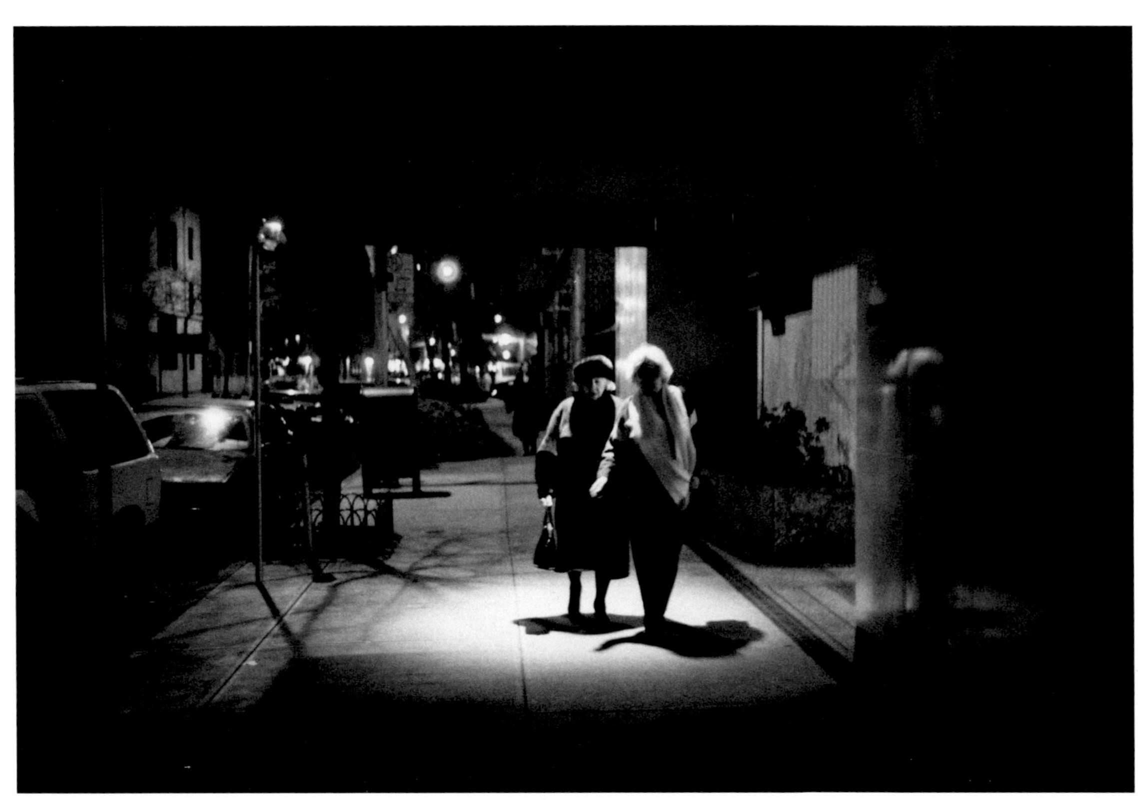

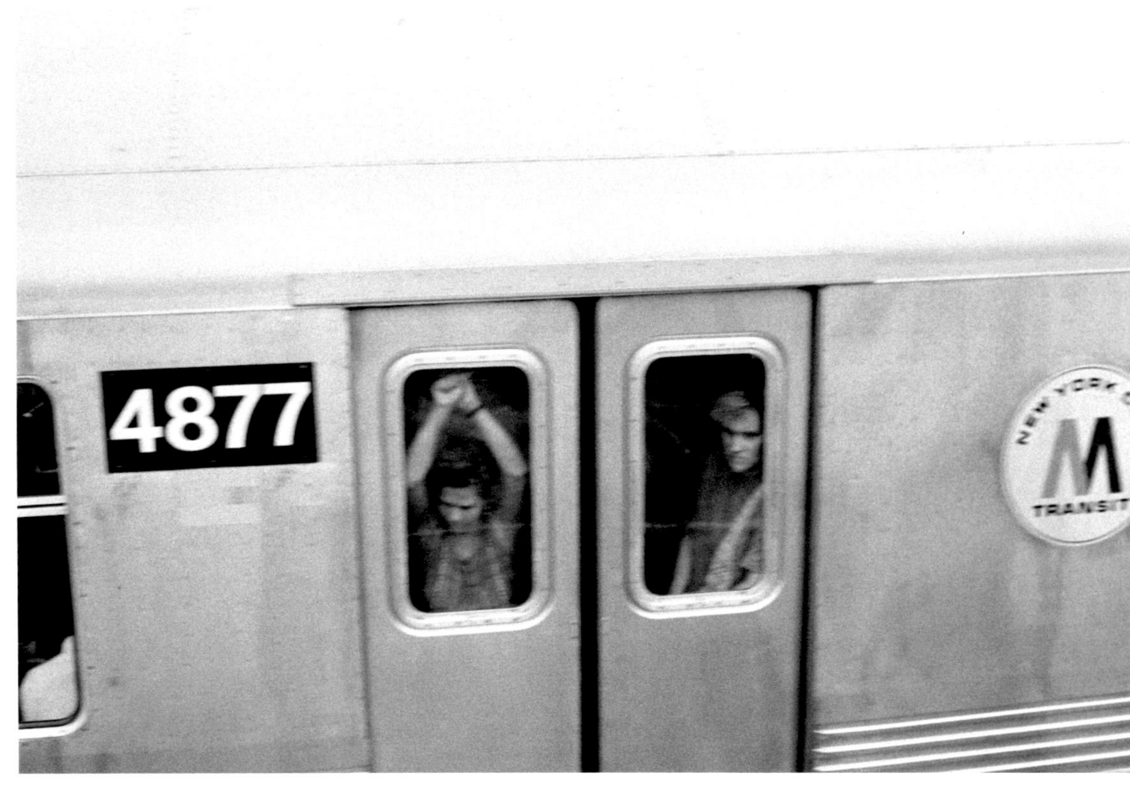

4877
NEW YORK CITY
TRANSIT

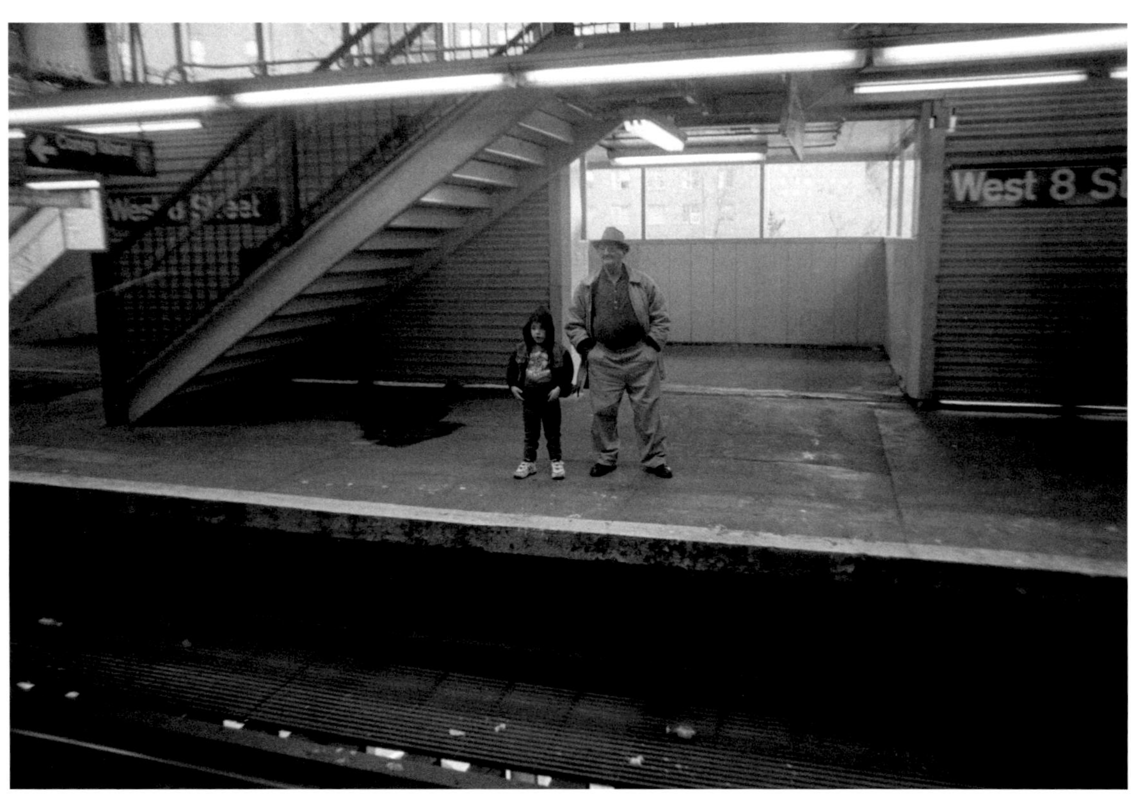
West 8 Street
West 8 St

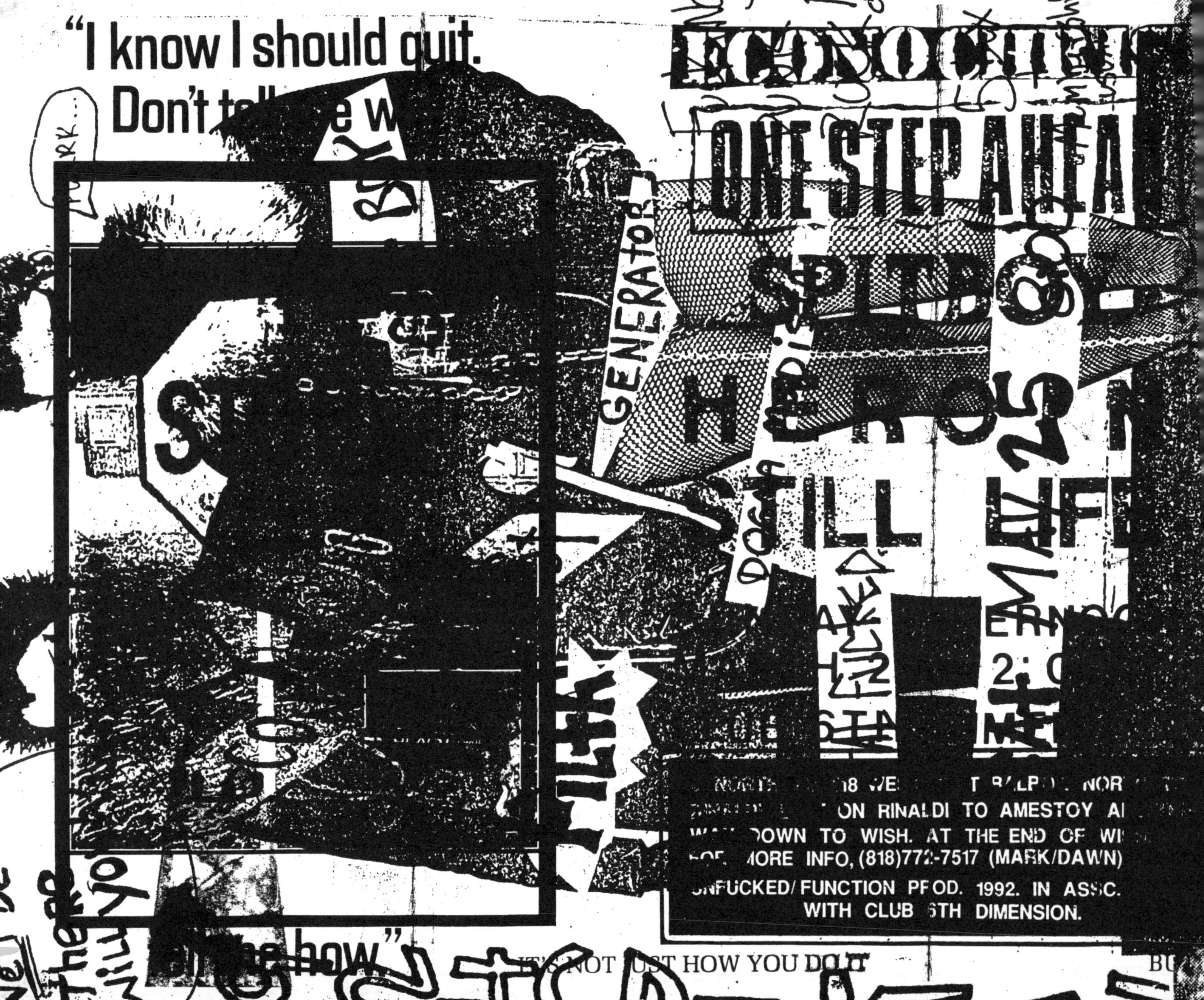

"I know I should quit.
Don't tell me w
ECONOCHRIST
ONE STEP AHEA
SPIT
GENERATOR
HEROS
ILL
MAY 25
somehow"
NORTH 18 WE T RALP NOR
ON RINALDI TO AMESTOY A
DOWN TO WISH. AT THE END OF WI
FOR MORE INFO, (818)772-7517 (MARK/DAWN)
NFUCKED/ FUNCTION PROD. 1992. IN ASSC.
WITH CLUB 6TH DIMENSION.
IT'S NOT JUST HOW YOU DO IT
BU